DRAWING IS EASY!

DRAWING FLOWERS, TREES, AND PLANTS

Written & designed by Anton Poitier

Illustrated by Hui Yuan Chang

Published in 2022 by Windmill Books,
an Imprint of Rosen Publishing
29 East 21st Street, New York, NY 10010

Illustrated by: Hui Yuan Chang

Cataloging-in-Publication Data

Names: Poitier, Anton, author. | Chang, Hui Yuan, illustrator.
Title: Drawing flowers, trees, and plants / written by Anton Poitier, illustrated by Hui Yuan Chang.
Description: New York : Windmill Books, 2022. | Series: Drawing is easy!
Identifiers: ISBN 9781499487305 (pbk.) | ISBN 9781499487329 (library bound) | ISBN 9781499487312 (6 pack) | ISBN 9781499487336 (ebook)
Subjects: LCSH: Flowers in art--Juvenile literature. | Plants in art--Juvenile literature. | Botanical illustration--Technique--Juvenile literature. | Drawing--Technique--Juvenile literature.
Classification: LCC NC805.P65 2022 | DDC 743.6--dc23

Printed in the United States of America

CPSIA Compliance Information: Batch BSWM22: For Further Information contact Rosen Publishing, New York, New York at 1-800-237-9932

WINDMILL BOOKS

Let's get started!

This book shows you how to draw flowers, trees, and plants by drawing shapes. There are steps to follow, and lots of hints and tips for making your drawings different!

Get drawing!

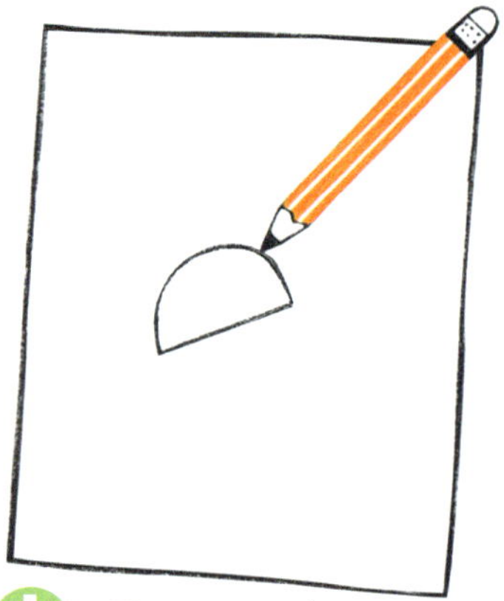

1 Begin by drawing the first shape in the center of a piece of paper.

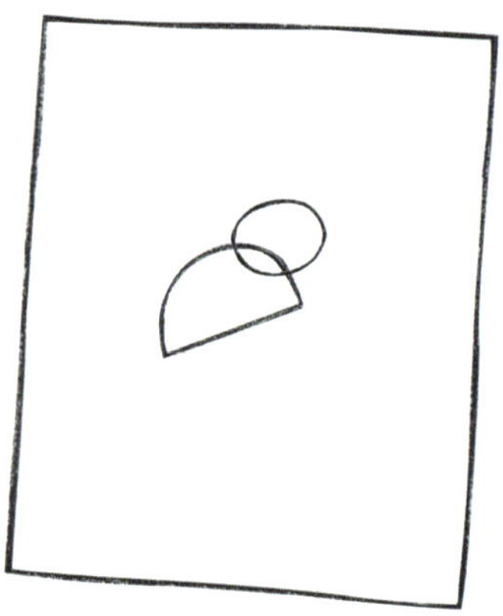

2 Draw the second shape where shown.

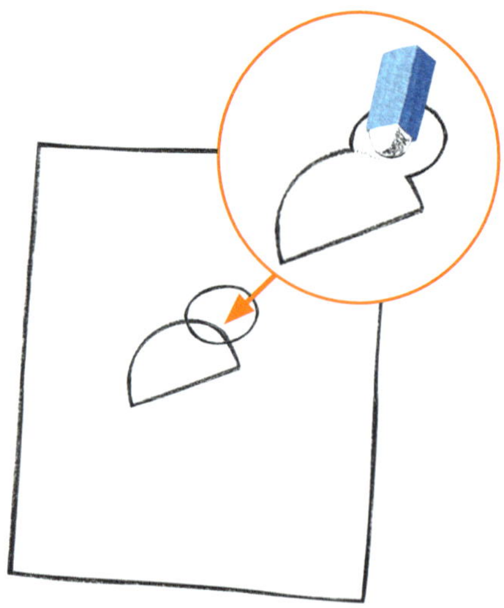

3 Erase the pencil marks where they overlap.

Tips to make your drawings special

Choose colors that suit each of the flowers, trees, and plants.

Bright colors

Pastel colors

Add a vase for your flowers. There are ideas on the last page.

Coloring your pictures

Here are some handy tips. You can use colored pencils, felt-tip pens, crayons, or watercolor paints to complete your drawing. Water-soluble colored pencils work very well. The pictures in this book are colored in this way.

Blend the pencil colors with water.

Paint over the pencil with water.

Use the same color all over, then use a darker pencil to pick out the details.

Use markers for tiny details.

Color around flowers to make them stand out in white.

Draw a daffodil

1 Draw the corona.

2 Now draw the back of the corona.

3 Add the first petal.

4 Continue adding petals.

5 Draw the stem.

6 Add a leaf.

7 Draw another leaf.

Draw a daffodil garden!

Add some mud to make a garden.

Change the direction of your daffodil.

Draw a little mouse.

Draw a water lily

1 Draw the corona.

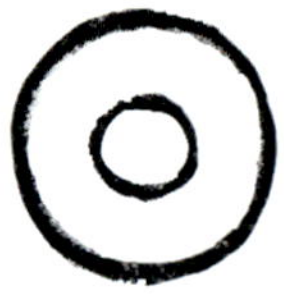

2 Next, draw all the small petals.

3 Add the large petals around the smaller ones.

4 Draw a stem.

5 Add some lily pads.

Draw some little frogs to sit on the water lilies.

Add some water too!

Make lots of water lilies!

Change the shape of a flower by drawing the petals so that they overlap.

Draw a rose

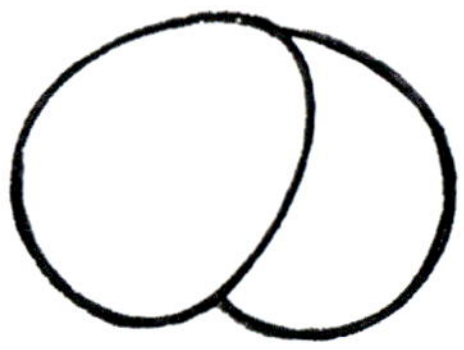

1 Draw the small petals.

2 Overlap the shapes like this.

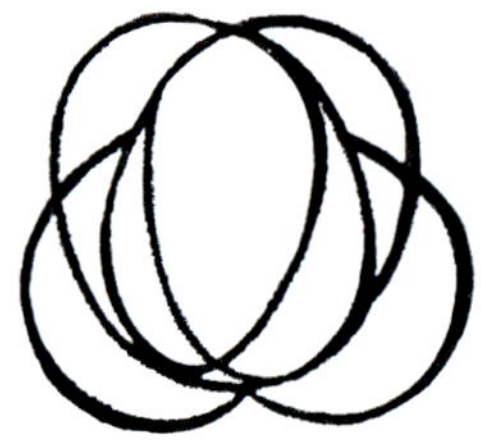

3 Overlap the shapes again.

4 Draw a heart shape to make the big petals.

5 Continue the petals all around the flower.

6 Add the stem and the sepal under the petals.

7 Draw two leaves about halfway down the stem.

Use pretty pinks and reds for the flowers, with green leaves.

Add a spiral in the center of the rose for a great effect!

Draw a pretty bow to make your flowers even prettier!

Draw a beautiful bunch of roses to give to a friend!

Draw a sunflower

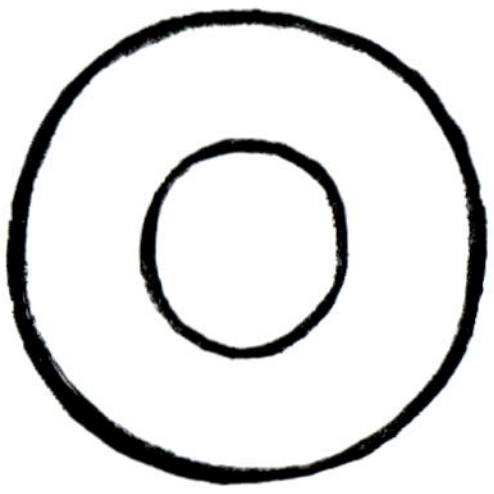

1 Draw the corona.

2 Add lots of petals all the way around the corona.

3 Draw the stem and two leaves.

Fill a vase with sunflowers!

Color in lots of little seeds in the center.

Draw a pretty dragonfly to make a summer picture!

Draw a colorful vase for your sunflowers.

Make a sunflower appear to be turning away.

Draw a tulip

1 Draw a petal.

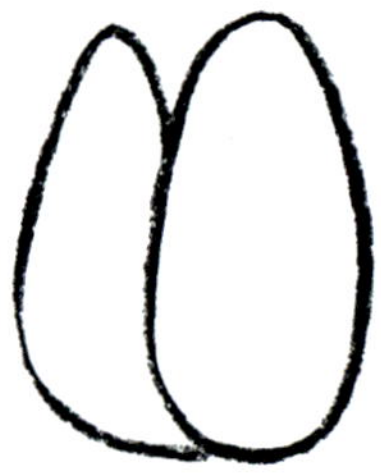

2 Add another petal.

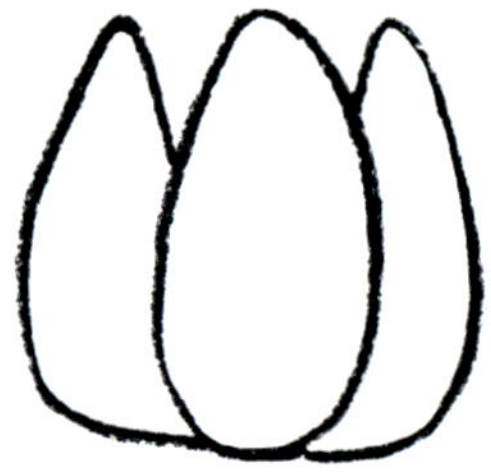

3 Draw a third petal.

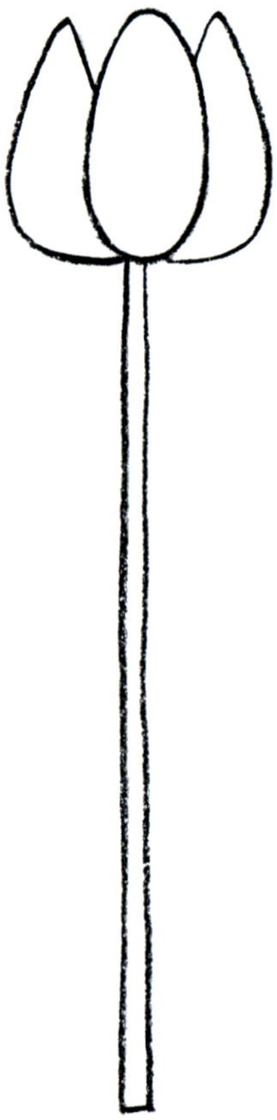

4 Add the stem.

5 Draw a leaf.

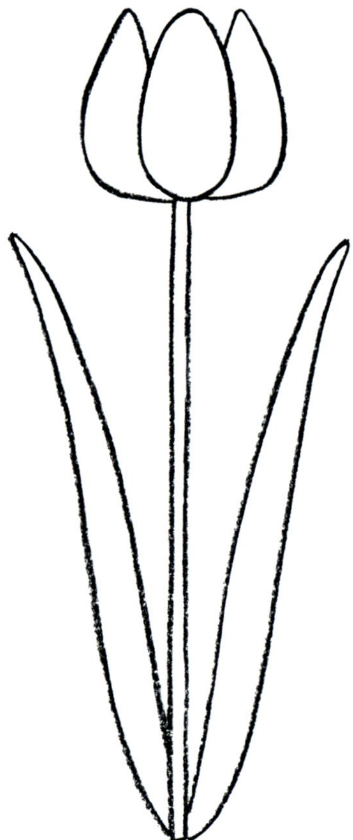

6 Draw another leaf.

Tulips are so colorful!

Use a semicircular shape to draw flowers that are more closed up.

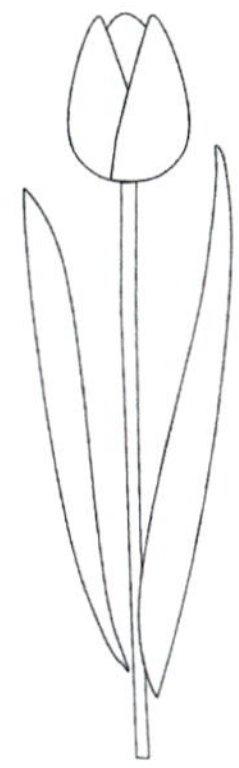

Use lots of colors!

Fill a vase with some open tulips and some that are more closed up.

Draw pine trees

1 Draw a triangle.

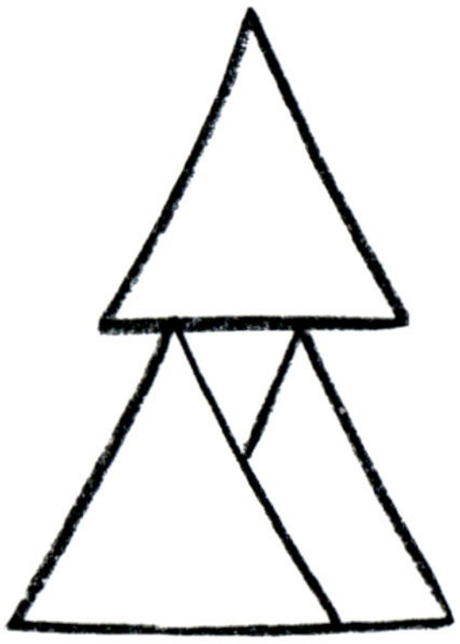

2 Add two more triangles.

3 Draw two more triangles to make the tree.

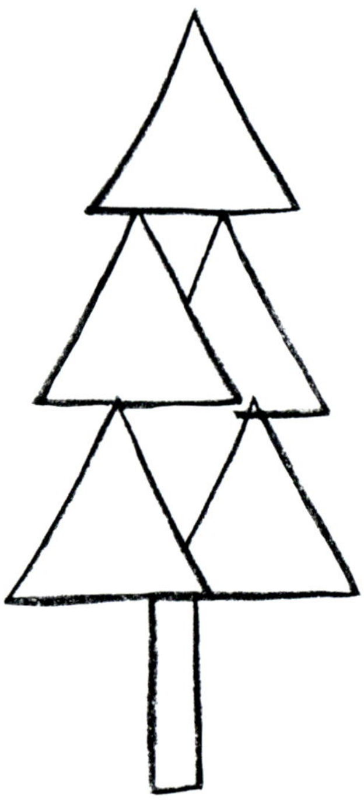

4 Add the trunk.

1 Draw a large triangle.

2 Add the trunk.

Draw a forest of different Christmas trees!

Draw presents too!

Decorate each tree.

Draw leafy trees

Draw two different trees like this:

1 Draw the leafy part sideways.

2 Add the trunk.

1 Draw the leafy part lengthways.

2 Add the trunk.

Imagine all the animals in the woods!

Add a bear and some birds.

Make each tree different.

Draw a lion too!

Draw a butterfly garden

1 Draw the butterfly's body.

2 Add a top wing.

3 Draw the other top wing.

4 Add a bottom wing.

5 Draw the other bottom wing.

Create lots of butterflies for your garden!

Color each butterfly with a different pattern.

Use lots of colors.

Draw flowers at the bottom of the paper and butterflies above.

Draw a palm tree

1 Draw two leaves on the left.

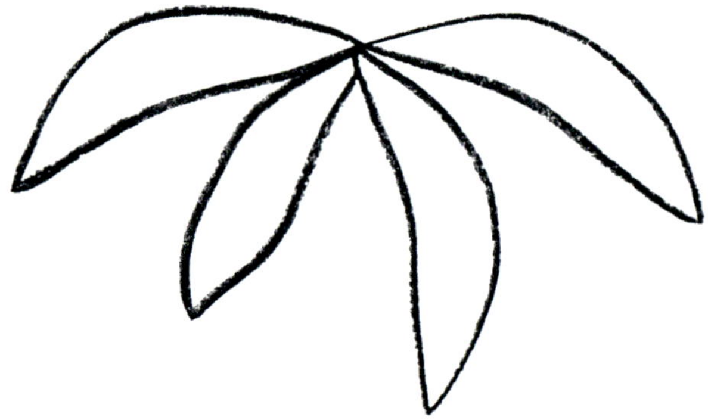

2 Add two leaves on the right.

3 Now draw three leaves at the top.

4 Draw the trunk.

Use different shades of green for the leaves.

Draw lots of palm trees so that they overlap.

Imagine a desert island for your palms!

Draw a daisy and a bee

Draw a daisy like this:

1 Draw the corona.

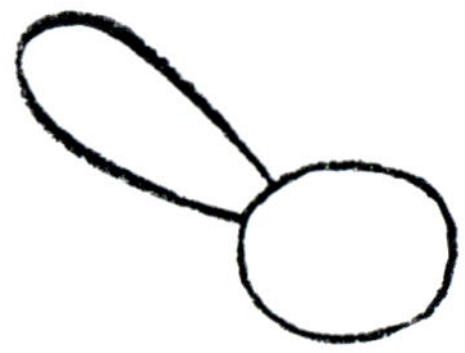

2 Add a petal.

3 Add more petals all the way around the corona.

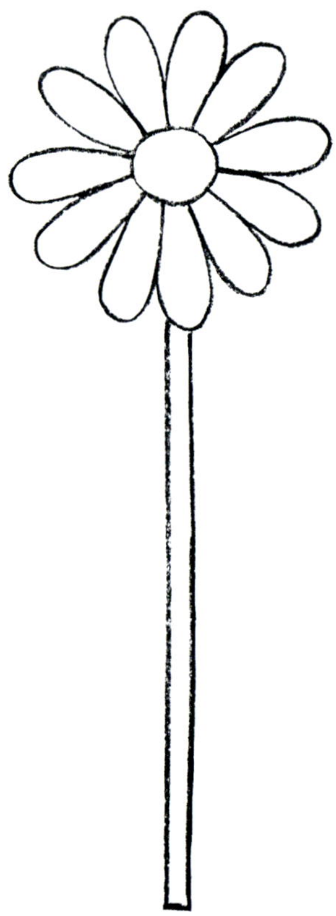

4 Add the stem.

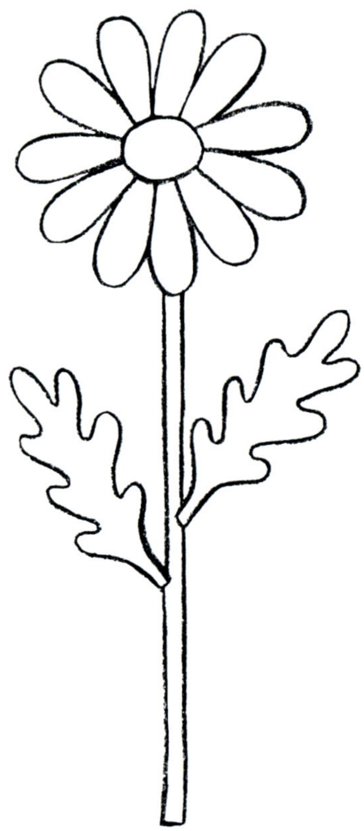

5 Draw the leaves.

Draw a bee:

1

Draw the head.

2

Add the body.

3

Draw a wing.

4

Draw the other wing.

Be a busy bee and draw this garden!

Color around the white petals to make them stand out.

Draw several bees.

Draw a closed flower.

Draw buttercups

1. Draw a large petal.

2. Overlap a small petal.

3. Add a heart-shaped petal.

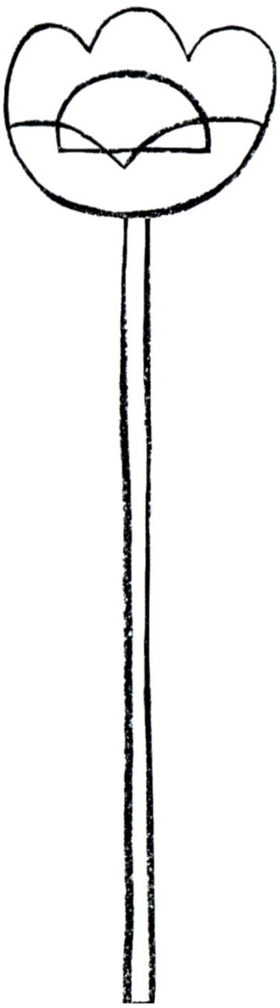

4. Add the stem.

5. Draw a leaf on one side of the stem.

Fill the background with blossoms!

Draw a field of buttercups and ladybugs!

Draw a flowering cactus

1 2 3 4 5

Draw the top half of the petal. Then follow the steps above to complete the flower shape.

6 Draw the cactus.

7 Add the smaller branches.

8 Draw more flowers.

Make a cactus garden with a lizard!

Make the cactus very prickly!

Use strong, bright colors.

You could draw the flower half hidden, like this.

Add a friendly lizard!

Water the flowers

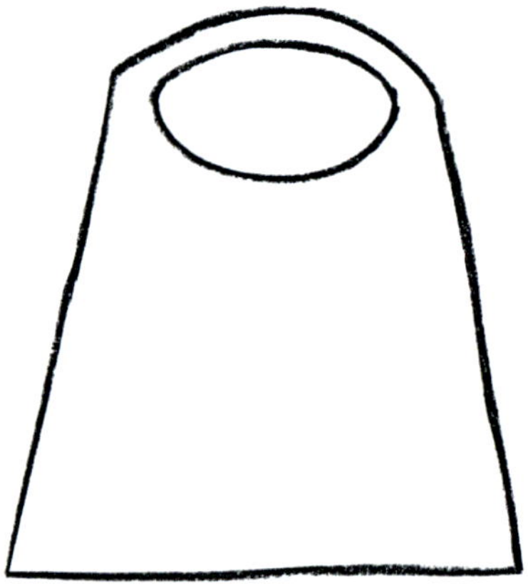

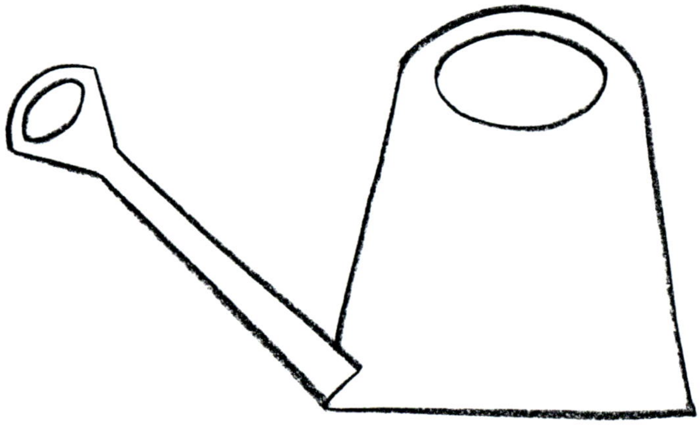

1 Draw the watering can.

2 Add the spout.

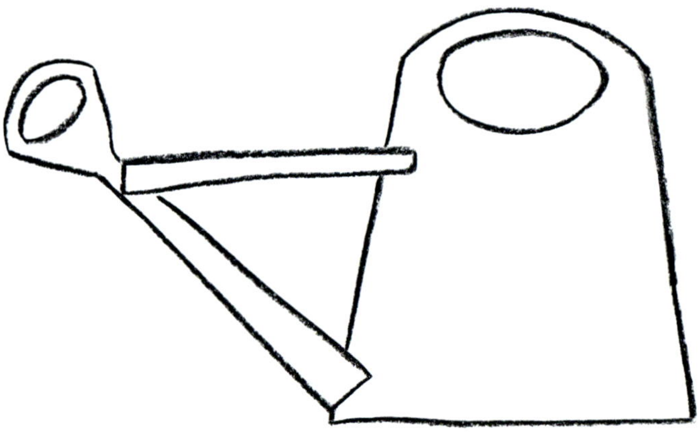

3 Draw the part that holds the spout.

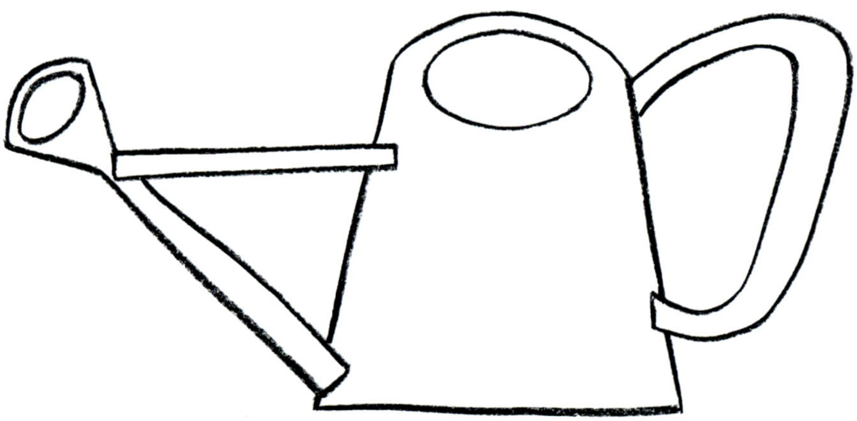

4 Add the handle.

Water your plants every day!

Add birds to your scene.

Plants look good
in watering cans!

Fill the page
with color!

Draw a poppy

1 Draw the poppy's center.

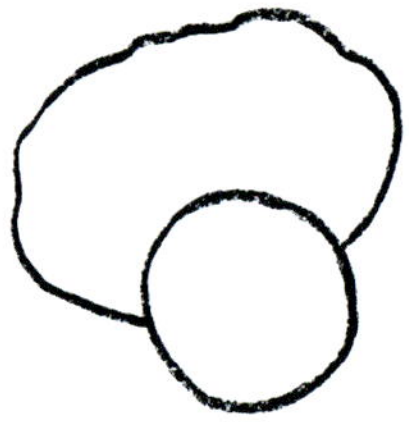

2 Add a petal.

3 Draw another petal.

4 Add a third petal.

5 Draw the fourth petal.

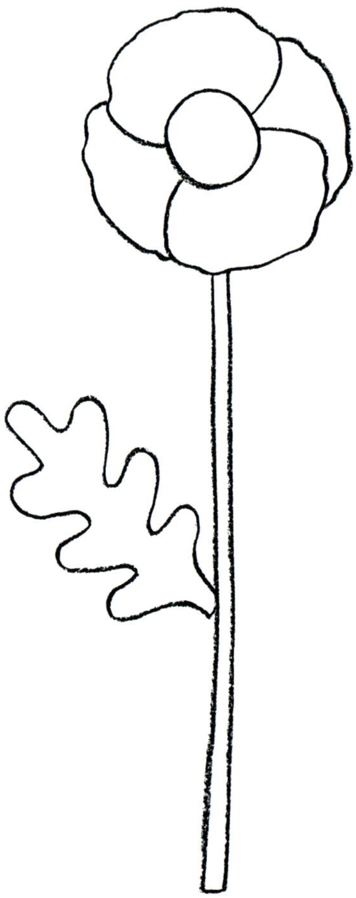

6 Add a stem and leaf.

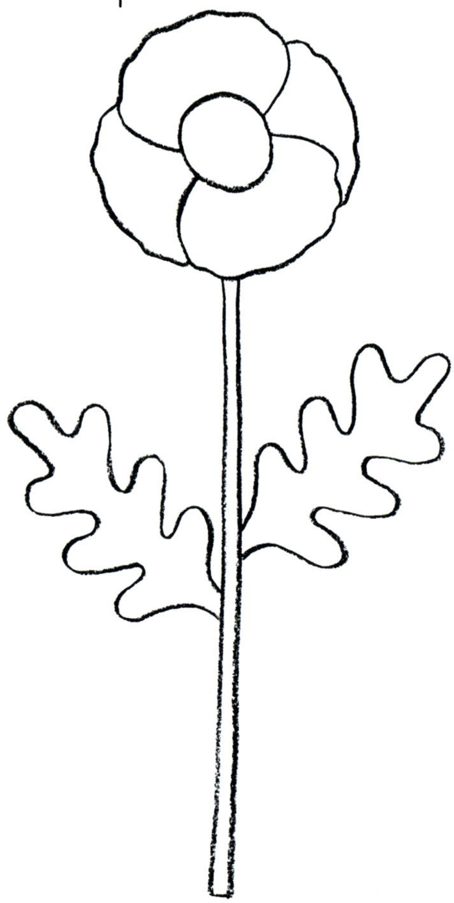

7 Then add another leaf.

Make a beautiful field of poppies!

Use two different greens for the leaves.

Make some poppies closed up.

Draw a pretty vase!

Draw half of a vase or pot shape any way you like, then draw the other half!

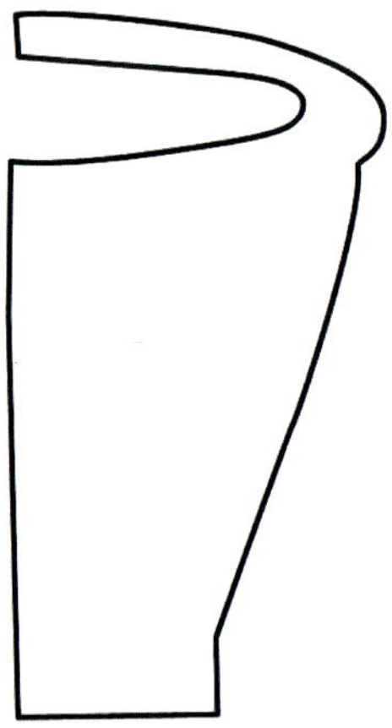

Make a pot with straight sides to go with a cactus.

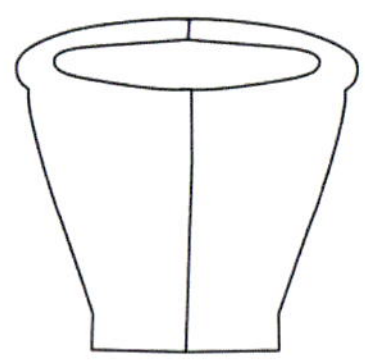

Draw patterns on your vase.

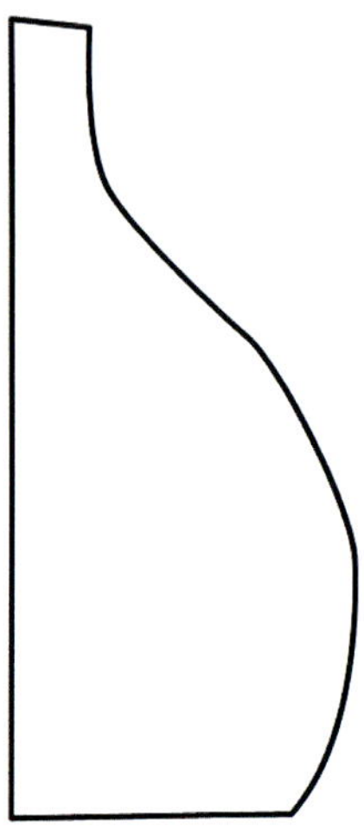

This curvy vase looks good with a single stem, such as a daisy.

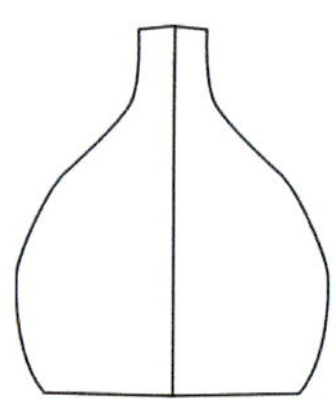

Stripes look good.

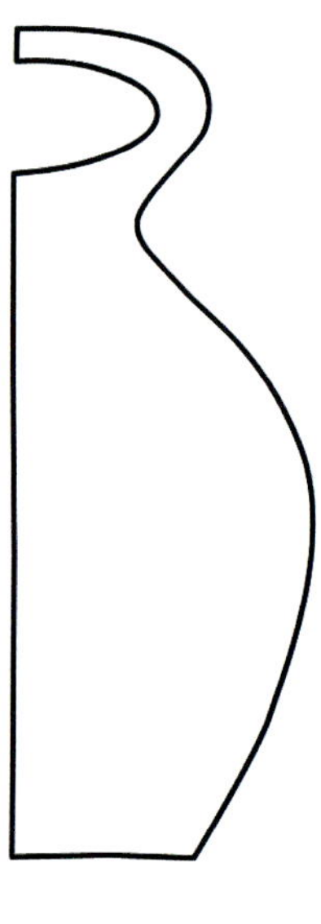

Try a nice sunflower in this lovely vase.

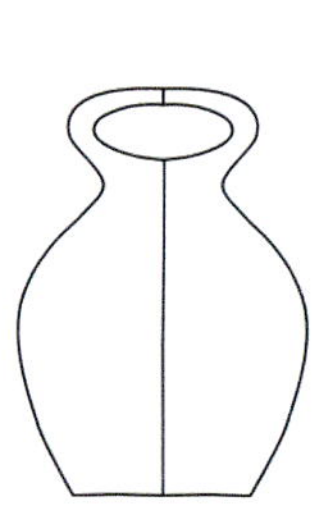

Color the inside darker.